Theodore Martin

Shakespeare or Bacon?

Theodore Martin

Shakespeare or Bacon?

ISBN/EAN: 9783337063665

Printed in Europe, USA, Canada, Australia, Japan

Cover: Foto ©Thomas Meinert / pixelio.de

More available books at **www.hansebooks.com**

SHAKESPEARE

OR

BACON?

BY

SIR THEODORE MARTIN, K.C.B.

WILLIAM BLACKWOOD AND SONS
EDINBURGH AND LONDON

SHAKESPEARE OR BACON?

SHAKESPEARE OR BACON?

BY

SIR THEODORE MARTIN, K.C.B.

REPRINTED FROM 'BLACKWOOD'S MAGAZINE'
WITH ADDITIONS

WILLIAM BLACKWOOD AND SONS
EDINBURGH AND LONDON
MDCCCLXXXVIII

SHAKESPEARE OR BACON?

"How one starts at the conjunction of the names of Bacon and Shakespeare! And how strange it seems that no other than a casual conjunction of their names should seem to exist, or should yet have been discovered!" So wrote Sir Henry Taylor (27th August 1870) to Mr James Spedding, adding an expression of his surprise that two of the world's greatest men should have lived at the same time and in the same city without to all appearance having known each other, or "leaving some mark and token of the knowledge." In his reply, four days afterwards, Mr Spedding says: "I see nothing surprising in the fact—for I take it to be a fact—that Bacon knew nothing about Shakespeare, and that he knew nothing of Bacon except his political writings and his popular reputation as a rising lawyer, of which there is no reason to suppose that he was

A

ignorant. Why should Bacon have known more of
Shakespeare than you do of Mark Lemon, or Planché,
or Morton? . . . I have no reason to think that
Bacon had ever seen or read anything of Shakespeare's
composition. 'Venus and Adonis' and the 'Rape of
Lucrece' are the most likely; but one can easily
imagine his reading them, and not caring to read anything else by the same hand."[1]

The study of a lifetime, devoted with enthusiasm to
a scrutiny of the writings and character of Bacon, and
guided by the light of a fine critical faculty and a
profound acquaintance with not only Shakespeare but
with every great English writer of the era of Elizabeth
and James, gives to these words of Mr Spedding a
weight beyond that of any writer of mark who has
dealt with this question before or since. No one can
say of him, that he did not know the literary characteristics of both Bacon and Shakespeare with all conceivable thoroughness. Neither can it be questioned, that
he of all men is entitled to speak with authority not
only of what Bacon could do or could not do as an
author, but also of what was possible for him to have
done, consistently with the occupations and necessities
of his life. This being so, when he states his convic-

---

[1] Sir Henry Taylor's Correspondence, pp. 306, 307. London: 1888.

tion that in all probability Bacon never read, nor even cared to read, the poems and dramas ascribed to Shakespeare, the mass of intelligent and cultivated students of our great poet will be disposed to adopt his opinion as conclusive. Who so likely as he to know what were Bacon's gifts, what his literary tastes, or to find in his austere and unemotional temperament no affinity to, or even sympathy with, the genius to which we owe the poems and the dramas which, as time has proved, were the noblest outcome of the literary activity of his age?

Nevertheless a creed directly at variance with that of Mr Spedding has sprung up in these last years. Its adherents, if not numerous, are at all events energetic, and so adventurous in assertion that they have created uneasiness in the minds of many who, loving Shakespeare, have yet never made themselves familiar with the ascertained facts of his life. To bring these facts and the general argument as to his right to the authorship—acknowledged in his lifetime, and ever since—shortly before readers of this class, seemed not undesirable, enabling them, as it will do, to justify the faith that is in them as to the Shakespearian authorship of the poems, the sonnets, and the plays. For very many, such an essay is of course superfluous; and the Baconian heresy, they may think, might well be allowed to wear itself out, like other heresies, from inherent weakness. But there is a large class who, having no foundation for their belief but inherited tradition, will not be sorry to learn on how sure a basis that belief may be rested. For them the following pages are written.

Bacon, in his second and last will, dated 19th December 1625, made an appeal to the charitable judgment of after times in these words—" For my name and memory I leave it to men's charitable speeches, and to foreign nations, and the next ages." He might well do so. The doubtful incidents of a shifty and in some particulars by no means exemplary life he might fairly suppose would be but little known to foreign nations and to men of future centuries. Time, to use his own words in a letter to Sir Humphrey May in 1625, would "have turned envy to pity;" and what was blameworthy in his life would, in any case, be judged lightly by posterity, in their gratitude for the treasures of profound observation and thought with which his name would be identified. "It is reason," as he writes in his essay "Of Nobility," that "the memory of men's virtues remain to their posterity, and their

faults die with themselves." Bacon died a few months
after making his will, on the 9th of April 1626.

No author probably ever set greater store upon the
produce of his brain, or was at more pains to see that
it was neither mangled nor misrepresented by careless
printing or editing. Neither is there the slightest
reason to believe that he did not take good care,—nay,
on the contrary, that he was not at especial pains to
ensure,—that the world should be informed of everything he had written, which he deemed worthy to be
preserved. Observe what care he took of his writings
in the sentences of his will next to those above quoted.
" *As to that durable part of my memory, which consisteth
in my works and writings,* I desire my executors, and
especially Sir John Constable and my very good friend
Mr Bosville, to take care that of all my writings, both
of English and of Latin, there may be books fair bound,
and placed in the King's library, and in the library of the
University of Cambridge, and in the library of Trinity
College, where myself was bred, and in the library
of the University of Oxonford, and in the library of
my Lord of Canterbury, and in the library of Eaton." [1]

Two years before Bacon made his final will, the first
or 1623 folio of Shakespeare's plays was published,

---

[1] Spedding's Life and Letters of Bacon, vol. vii. p. 539.

with the following title-page : "*Mr William Shake-speare's Comedies, Histories, and Tragedies; Published according to the True Originall Copies. London: Printed by Isaac Jaggard and Ed. Blount.* 1623." It was a portly volume of nearly a thousand pages, and must have taken many months, probably the best part of a year, to set up in types and get printed off. The printing of similar folios in those days was marked by anything but exemplary accuracy. But this volume abounds to such excess in typographical flaws of every kind, that the only conclusion in regard to it which can be drawn is, that the printing was not superintended by any one competent to discharge the duty of the printing-house "reader" of the present day, but was suffered to appear with "all the imperfections on its head," which distinguish "proof-sheets" as they issue from the hands of careless or illiterate compositors. Most clearly the proof-sheets of this volume had never been read by any man of literary skill, still less by any man capable of rectifying a blundered text. In this respect the book offers a marked contrast to the text of Bacon's Works, printed in his own time, which were revised and re-revised till they were brought up to a finished perfection.[1]

[1] In partial proof of this, it is only necessary to refer to the Notes appended by Mr Aldis Wright to his admirable edition of the Essays,

Down to the year 1856 the world was content to accept as truth the statement of the folio of 1623, that it contained the plays of Mr William Shakespeare " according to the true original copies." To the two preceding centuries and a half the marvel of Shakespeare's genius had been more or less vividly apparent. His contemporaries had acknowledged it; and as the years went on, and under reverent study that marvel became more deeply felt, men were content to find the solution of it in the fact, that the birth of these masterpieces of dramatic writing was due—only in a higher degree—to the same heaven-sent inspiration to which great sculptors, painters, warriors, and statesmen owe their pre-eminence. How often has it been seen that men of genius, without the long and painful culture of school teaching, have, amid the bustle of active life, by promiscuous reading, by intercourse with their fellow-men, by quick and almost unconscious intuition, acquired with marvellous ease great stores of knowledge, which they have brought to bear upon and to illustrate the conceptions of their imagination and fancy! Knowing this, men would not set a limit to " the gifts that God gives," or see anything more strange in the prodigality

published by Macmillan & Co. in 1862. So sensitive about accuracy and finish was Bacon, that he transcribed, altering as he wrote, his ' Novum Organum' twelve, and his 'Advancement of Learning' seven times.

of power in observation, in feeling, in humour, in
thought, and in expression, as shown by the son of
the Stratford-on-Avon wool-stapler, than in the kin-
dred manifestations of genius in men as lowly born,
and as little favoured in point of education as he, of
which biographical records furnish countless instances.[1]

But in 1856, or thereabouts, a new light dawned
upon certain people, to whom the ways of genius were
a stumbling-block. The plays, they conceived, could
not have been written by a man of lowly origin, of
scanty education, a struggling actor, who had the
prosaic virtue of looking carefully after his pounds,
shillings, and pence, and who, moreover, was content
to retire, in the fulness of his fame, with a moderate
competence, to the small country town where he was
born, and to leave his plays to shift for themselves
with posterity, in seemingly perfect indifference whether
they were printed or not printed, remembered or buried

[1] For example.—Giotto, a shepherd boy; Leonardo da Vinci, the
illegitimate son of a common notary; Marlowe, the son of a shoemaker;
Ben Jonson, posthumous son of a clergyman, but brought up by a
bricklayer stepfather; Massinger, the son of a nobleman's servant;
Burns, the son of a small farmer; Keats, an apothecary's apprentice,
and the son of a livery-stable-keeper; Turner, a barber's son. The
list may be extended indefinitely of men who, with all external odds
against them, have triumphed far beyond those who had all these odds
in their favour.

in oblivion. This virtue of modesty and carelessness of fame is so unlike the characteristic of "the mob of gentlemen who write with ease," at all times, and especially in these our days—it is so hard to be understood by people possessed by small literary ambitions, that it was natural it should be regarded by them as utterly incomprehensible. So they set themselves to look elsewhere for the true author. Shakespeare lived amid a crowd of great dramatic writers—Peele, Marlowe, Greene, Jonson, Dekker, Lyly, Marston, Chapman, Beaumont and Fletcher, Middleton, and others. But we know their works; and to ascribe "Othello," "Macbeth," "Romeo and Juliet," "Julius Cæsar," "King Lear," or the other great plays, to any of them, would have been ridiculous. Outside this circle, therefore, the search had to be made; but outside it there was no choice. Only Francis Bacon towered pre-eminently above his literary contemporaries. He, and he only, therefore, could have written the immortal dramas! And so the world was called upon to forego its old belief in the marvel that one man had written Shakespeare's plays, and to adopt a creed which implied a marvel far greater still, adding these plays as it did to the other massive and voluminous acknowledged works of Francis, Lord Verulam—in themselves enough, and more than enough, to have absorbed the leisure and exhausted the energies of the most vigorous intellect. The great jurist, statesman, philosopher, and natural historian of his age was, according to this new doctrine, also the greatest dramatist of any age!

Who has the merit of being first in the field with this astounding discovery is not very clear. America claims to have been first in the person of Mr J. C. Hart, who, in his book 'The Romance of Yachting,' published at New York in 1848, is said to have thrown a doubt on Shakespeare's authorship. England, however, was not far behind; for in September 1856, a Mr William Henry Smith propounded similar doubts in a letter to Lord Ellesmere, sometime President of the then Shakespeare Society, which, as the copy before us bears, was modestly printed for private circulation. Mr Smith had really little else to say for his theory beyond his own personal impression that Shakespeare, by birth, education, and pursuits, was not the kind of man to write the plays; while Bacon had "all the necessary qualifications—a mind well stored by study and enlarged by travel, with a comprehensive knowledge of nature, men, and books." But if Bacon wrote the plays, why did he not say so? Mr Smith's answer to this very obvious question was the wholly gratuitous assumption, that to have been known to write plays, or to have business relations with actors, would have been ruinous to Bacon's prospects at the Bar and in Parliament; and that, being driven into the avocation of dramatist by the necessity of eking out his income, he got Shakespeare to lend his name as a blind to the real authorship! To be a great dramatic writer, and yet to go through life without being suspected of the gifts that go to make one, would to ordinary minds seem to be as impossible as to be born with the genius of a Phidias or a Titian, and not to show it. But such a thing as the irrepressible impulse of dramatic genius to find expression in its only possible medium is not even suggested by Mr Smith as among Bacon's motives. He claims for him, indeed, " great dramatic talent," on the strength of the very flimsy masques and pageants in which Bacon is known to have had a share, and of some vague record, that " he could assume the most different characters, and speak the language proper to each with a facility which was perfectly natural "—a gift which might have produced a Charles Matthews, senior, and is in itself by no means uncommon, but which would go but a very little way towards the invention of a single scene of even the weakest of the Shakespearian plays.

Strangely enough, Mr Smith, unable apparently to
foresee to what his argument led, appealed to the first
folio in proof of his assumption. "Bacon," he writes,
"was disgraced in 1621, and immediately set himself
to collect and revise his literary works." "Immediately" is rather a strong assertion, but he no doubt
very soon busied himself in literary and scientific work.
He finished his 'Life of Henry VII.,' and set to work
upon the completion and translation into Latin of his
'Advancement of Learning,' which appeared in October
1623 as 'De Augmentis Scientiarum.'[1] In the same
year he published his 'History of the Winds' and his
'Treatise on Death and Life.' At this time, as his
correspondence proves, he was busy with anything but
poetry or play-books.[2] In March 1622 he offered to
draw up a digest of the law, a project which he had
long cherished, and showed the greatest anxiety to get

[1] "Modern language will, at one time or another," he wrote to Mr
Tobie Matthews in June 1623, "play the bankrupt with books; and
since I have lost much time with this age, I shall be glad, as God will
give me leave, to recover it with posterity." Surely this is about the
very last thought that would be uppermost in a mind that had conceived such plays as Shakespeare's, and was then passing, or had just
passed, the first folio through the press.

[2] As to how Bacon was occupied in 1622, see his letter to the Bishop
of Winchester, Spedding's 'Life and Works of Bacon,' vol. vii. p. 371
et seq., and his letter to Father Redemptor Baranzano (ibid., p. 375 et
seq.)

back into active political life. He was, moreover, in wretched health, but at the same time intent on making progress with his 'Instauratio Magna,' with all the eagerness of a man who feared that his life would be cut short before he could accomplish the chief object of his ambition. All his occupations during 1622-23, during which the first Shakespeare folio was at press, are thus fully accounted for.

"But," continues Mr Smith, "in 1623 a folio of thirty-six plays (including some, and excluding others, which had always been reputed Shakespeare's) was published." And then he asks, in the triumphant emphasis of italics, " Who but the author himself could have exercised this power of discrimination ?" As if the researches of Shakespearian students had not demonstrated to a certainty, that one of the chief defects of the folio was the absence of this very "power of discrimination," which, if duly exercised, would, besides giving us a sound text, have shown which of these plays were all Shakespeare's, and which had only been worked up into their present form, upon the slight or clumsy fabric of some inferior hand.

It is characteristic of the inexact and illogical kind of mind which had persuaded itself of the soundness of a theory based on such trivial data, that Mr Smith

accepted without verification the "remarkable words,"
as he calls them, to be found in Bacon's will. "My
name and memory I leave to foreign nations; and to
my own countrymen, *after some time be passed over*,"
—language which, it may be presumed, in the light of
the use which has since been made of it, was held by
Mr Smith to point to some revelation of great work
done by Bacon, which should be divulged to the world,
"after some time had passed over." Unluckily for
this theory, the words in italics do not exist in the
will.[1] Nevertheless, followers in Mr Smith's wake
have found them so convenient for their theory, that
they repeat the misquotation, and ignore the actual
words of Bacon's last will, to which reference has
already been made.

Mr Smith seems never to have perceived that, if
Bacon were indeed the author of the plays, and revised the first folio, or, as we should say, saw it through
the press, he was guilty of inconceivable carelessness in
letting it go forth with thousands of mortal blunders in
the text, "the least a death" to prosody, poetry, and

---

[1] Bacon made two wills, one in 1621 after his impeachment, and one
in 1625; but in neither do the words quoted in italics appear. The
words of the will of 1621 are, "I bequeath my name to the next ages
and to foreign nations."

sound printing.[1] The man, in short, who rewrote and
retouched over and over even so relatively small a book
as his Essays, was content to leave innumerable blunders in passages of the finest poetry and the choicest
humour in all literature! What wonder if Shakespearian scholars, indeed the world generally, met the
preposterous assumption with the words of Horace—

" Quodcunque ostendis mihi sic, incredulus odi"!

Neither were they disposed to alter their opinion,
when America in the same year, 1856, sent forth an
apostle to preach the same new doctrine in the person of
a Miss Delia Bacon, to whom years of study of Shakespeare's works had revealed in them "a continuous
inner current of the philosophy of Sir Walter Raleigh,
and the imperishable thoughts of Lord Bacon." This
was Miss Bacon's first opinion. It seems to have been
modified when she came to grapple more closely with
the subject in a portentous volume of 582 pages
octavo—' The Philosophy of the Plays of Shakespeare
Unfolded,1857 '—in which, dropping Sir Walter Raleigh
out of the discussion, she ascribed the whole honour and
glory of the thirty-seven plays to her namesake. Poor

---

[1] The typographical errors alone have been computed to amount to
nearly 20,000.

Miss Bacon died a victim to her own belief. She had
pondered over it until her brain gave way, and she
went to her grave possessed by her monomania. Of
course she had followers. What crazy enthusiast has
not? for there is a charm to a certain order of minds
in running counter to the established creeds of ordinary
mortals. Her mantle was not suffered to fall neglected.
She was quickly succeeded by a more vigorous, but
even more long-winded preacher of the same doctrine,
in Judge Nathaniel Holmes of Kentucky, who spent
696 octavo pages in demonstrating that Shakespeare
was utterly incapable of writing either poetry or plays,
being nothing but an illiterate stroller, who could
scarcely write his own name, who had no ambition but
to make money, and was not very scrupulous as to how
he made it; while Bacon was endowed with every
quality, natural and acquired, which was requisite for
the composition of the famous plays. Like Mr Smith,
Judge Holmes deals largely in assumptions—such, for
example, as that " it is historically known that Lord
Bacon wrote plays and poems." How " historically
known" he does not say, as neither by his contemporaries nor by the collectors of Elizabethan and Jaco-
bean poetry is he credited with that faculty. He left
behind him, it is true, a frost-bitten metrical version of

seven of the Psalms, written within a year or two of his
death, which scarcely rises to the Sternhold and Hopkins
level, published, when he was quite broken in health, in
1624; and one small poem, "The Retired Courtier," not
without beauty, and a paraphrased translation from the
Greek, have also been assigned to him on doubtful
authority.[1]

Very different from the doctrine of Mr Holmes was
the view taken by Mr James Spedding, who, by his fine
literary taste and deep study of Shakespeare, as well as
by the intimate knowledge of Bacon's mind and modes
of thought and expression gained in editing his works,
was entitled, as already said, to speak upon the subject
with authority.   Judge Holmes had courted his judgment, and this was his answer :—

"To ask me to believe that Bacon was the author of these
plays, is like asking me to believe that Lord Brougham was
the author, not only of Dickens's works, but of Thackeray's
and Tennyson's besides. That the author of 'Pickwick'
was Charles Dickens I know upon no better authority than
that upon which I know that the author of 'Hamlet' was a
man called William Shakespeare. And in what respect is
the one more difficult to believe than the other ? . . . If

---

[1] In the Appendix (p. 63) will be found specimens of these Psalms,
and also the only poems which have been assumed, but never proved,
to have been written by Bacon.

you had fixed upon anybody else rather than Bacon as the
true author—anybody of whom I know nothing—I should
have been scarcely less incredulous. But if there were any
reason for supposing that the real author was somebody else,
I think I am in a condition to say that, whoever it was, it
was not Francis Bacon. The difficulties which such a sup-
position would involve would be innumerable and altogether
insurmountable." [1]

Such a judgment from such a man is death to all
the arguments drawn by Mr Holmes and others from
fanciful parallelisms or analogies between passages in
Bacon's writings and passages in the Shakespeare
dramas. No man in England or elsewhere was more
thoroughly conversant than Mr Spedding with the
works of both Bacon and Shakespeare, or more capable
of bringing a sound critical judgment to bear upon the
distinctive literary qualities of each. But even if this
were not so, it is notorious that arguments of this sort,
frequently resorted to as they are to support charges of
plagiarism, are utterly deceptive. Great ideas are the
common property of great minds, especially if, being
contemporaries, the men who clothe them in words are
living in the same general atmosphere of thought and
daily using the same vocabulary. How, indeed, should

---

[1] 'Authorship of Shakespeare,' by N. Holmes, ed. 1886, vol. ii.,
App., pp. 613, 617.

it be otherwise? The same incidents, the same pheno-
mena, the same conditions of social development, the
same human characteristics, are daily and hourly fur-
nishing to them the same stimulus to their imagination, the same materials for thought. Literary history
does undoubtedly present some remarkable instances of
authors expressing the same feeling or the same thought
in closely analogous language. But we venture to say
that every competent judge who will so "slander his
leisure" as to wade through the so-called parallelisms
cited by Miss Bacon, Mr Holmes, Mr Smith, Mrs Pott,
and other victims of the Baconian delusion, will come
to the conclusion that they are mostly far-fetched and
not unfrequently overstrained to the point of absurdity.
It would be quite as reasonable to maintain on such
evidence that Bacon borrowed from Shakespeare, as
that Shakespeare and Bacon were one.

It is obviously essential for the Baconians to set out
with the assumption that Shakespeare was an illiterate
boor. They say as much as that he was so from the
first and remained so to the last, and say it in language
extravagant and coarse in proportion to the utter reck-
lessness of assumption from which it springs. He was
a butcher's boy, they tell us; he could only have been
some two years at school; he was a sordid money-

lender; and so completely had his nature become,
"like the dyer's hand, subdued to what it [had once]
worked in," that when he returned, at near fifty, to
Stratford, he resumed with delight the trade of butcher,
wool - stapler, and usurer. The ascertained facts of
Shakespeare's life are few. Still some facts there are
which cannot be disputed, and which give the lie to
this scandalous assumption.

Shakespeare came of a good stock on both father
and mother's side. They held a good position in Stratford, and if at a later period they became poor, they
were undoubtedly in easy circumstances during the
boyhood of Shakespeare. There was in Stratford an
excellent grammar-school, to which they were certain
to have sent their son, when he reached the age, about
six, at which boys were usually entered there. What
the course of study pursued at this and similar schools
was is well known, and was pointed out in an admirable
series of papers by the late Professor Spencer Baynes
on "What Shakespeare learnt at School" in 'Fraser's
Magazine' in 1879-80.[1] It was very much the same
as that of the Edinburgh High School in the days of
our youth, and brought a boy up, by the time he

---

[1] The subject was again treated by Mr Baynes in his masterly paper
on Shakespeare in the last edition of the 'Encyclopædia Britannica.'

reached the age of twelve, to the reading of such
writers as Ovid, Cicero, and Virgil in Latin, and the
New Testament and some of the orators and tragedians
in Greek. To send their children to the school was
within the means of all but the poorest, which John
Shakespeare and Mary Arden unquestionably were
not ; and all that is known of them justifies the
conclusion that it is inconceivable they should have
allowed their son to want any advantage common to
boys of his class. Every presumption is in favour of
the view that they would not be behind their neigh-
bours in a matter of this sort. John Shakespeare, a
leading burgess, who had held high office in the local
government of Stratford, would never have exposed
himself to the reproach of his fellow-townsmen for
neglecting the education of his children. Desperate,
indeed, are the straits to which the Baconian theorists
are driven, when, without a particle of evidence, they
deny to Shakespeare the advantages within the reach
of the sons of the humblest householder in Stratford.

The next clearly ascertained fact which bears upon
this part of the question is the publication of the
"Venus and Adonis," when Shakespeare was in his
twenty-ninth year. Only in the previous year does
he come clearly into notice as a rising dramatist

and poet, there being, as admitted by his best bio-
grapher, Mr Halliwell-Phillips,[1] nothing known of his
history between his twenty-third and twenty-eighth
year, — an interval that Mr Halliwell-Phillips very
reasonably considers "must have been the chief period
of Shakespeare's literary education," which, when he
left Stratford, could not, he thinks, have been otherwise than imperfect.

Imperfect truly it might be, as indeed, in a certain
sense, of what education can it be said that it is not
imperfect ? But who can doubt that between the
age of fourteen, when Shakespeare's schooling probably came to an end, and the time he went to London,
he was imbibing stores of observation and knowledge
at every pore, not from books only, but from the men
and women round him, from the sights and sounds of a

----

[1] Let us here acknowledge the debt that all students of Shakespeare
owe to Mr J. O. Halliwell-Phillips for the invaluable information which
he has brought together in the two volumes of his 'Outlines of the
Life of Shakespeare,' of which the sixth edition, published by Messrs
Longmans in 1886, contains every ascertained fact concerning Shakespeare, his family, fortune, and pursuits. The book is a model of
painstaking inquiry, and contains no conclusions that are not based
upon judicial proof. We are not aware whether Mr Halliwell-Phillips
has published his views upon the Shakespeare-Bacon controversy ; but
that he regards the proposition that Bacon wrote the plays, and the
arguments on which it is founded, as "lunacy," we have direct means
of knowing.

country life, and from the impulses that come to a
thoughtful and poetic mind in the solitude of its quiet
hours. Then it was, no doubt, that he grew familiar
with the woods, the brooks, the streams, the flowers,
the legends, the quaint local phrases, the songs, the
oddities of character, the sense of maidenly and
matronly charm, the visions of higher and better
things, that enrich the dreams of young imagination,
and which were afterwards to fill his pages with a
boundless wealth of suggestion and of illustration.
Then, too, he would be learning to apply this knowledge to what he had gathered from his favourite
books. This would be the time, in short, when he
was "making himself," as it was said of Sir Walter
Scott that he did, in the days before the Wizard of
the North revealed his magic to the world in the
poems and the novels which after middle age he
poured out in marvellous profusion.

Such, we know, was the view taken by Professor
Baynes, whose experience had satisfied him how true
it is, that it is not at school but by his own self-im-
posed studies afterwards that a man is educated, and
who so far differs from Mr Halliwell-Phillips as to
maintain, that before Shakespeare left Stratford he had
probably written the "Venus and Adonis," quoting in

support of his view the language of the dedication to
the Earl of Southampton, in which Shakespeare speaks
of it as " the first heir of his invention." It might
be so, for Shakespeare was twenty-one when he was
forced to leave Stratford; and, weighted although the
" Venus and Adonis " is with thought as well as passion, the genius which produced the dramas might
even at that early age have conceived and written it.
But however this may be, the poem shows a knowledge of what Ovid had written upon the same theme,
in a poem of which there existed at that time no English translation, which could not have been accidental,
any more than the language in which that knowledge
was expressed could have been within the command of
an uneducated man. Moreover, that Shakespeare knew
Latin, when or however acquired matters little, is
conclusively proved by his placing as motto upon the
title-page the following lines from Ovid's Elegies, the
very selection of which showed that, at this early date,
he set the calling of a poet above all ordinary objects
of ambition :—

> " Vilia miretur vulgus; mihi flavus Apollo
> Pocula Castalia plena ministret aqua."

May it not also be fairly argued, from the very selec-

tion of the subject, as well as from the manner in which
it is treated, that the youthful poet's mind had already
caught the classical tone, which he could only have
done through a considerable familiarity with some at
least of the Latin writers ? When we remember what
Keats was able to do in his " Ode to a Grecian Urn "
and his " Hyperion," despite his " small Latin and less
Greek," it is no wonder if Shakespeare turned his limited
knowledge of these languages to the excellent account
he did, and satisfied the scholarly men of his time that
he was well entitled to choose for " the first heir of his
invention " the motto, which it would have been imper-
tinence in a writer to select who had not a fair knowledge of the language in which it was written.

That they were satisfied of this, is tolerably evident,
for the success of the poem was immediate. Edition
followed edition, and by 1602 five had been printed.
In 1594 the " Lucrece," also dedicated to Lord Southampton, appeared, and ran into several editions. This
poem, like the " Venus and Adonis," bears internal
proofs of familiarity with what had been written by
Ovid on the same theme. Unless, therefore, it can be
shown that Shakespeare, who claimed the authorship
on the title-pages, did not write either poem, the charge
of want of education must fall to the ground. But

how can this be shown in the face of the fact that his
was by this time a familiar name among literary men
in London, some of whom would have been glad
enough to expose so glaring an imposture, while by
several of them his merits were recognised in such
epithets as " honey-tongued Shakespeare" (John Wee-
ver, 1595), "mellifluous and honey-tongued Shakespeare" (Francis Meres, 1598); and while "his sugared
sonnets," then unpublished, but which had probably
for many years been "circulating among his private
friends," were acknowledged by Meres as adding fresh
lustre to a name that had already been coupled with
many popular plays—"Midsummer Night's Dream,"
"The Merchant of Venice," "King John," and "Romeo
and Juliet" among the number ? [1]

Now it is to be borne in mind that Meres, from

---

[1] "As the soul of Euphorbus was thought to live in Pythagoras, so
the sweet witty soul of Ovid lives in mellifluous and honey-tongued
Shakespeare. Witness his 'Venus and Adonis'; his 'Lucrece'; his
sugared sonnets among his private friends, &c. As Plautus and Seneca
are accounted the best for comedy and tragedy among the Latins, so
Shakespeare among the English is the most excellent in both kinds for
the stage. . . . As Epius Stolo said that the Muses would speak
with Plautus's tongue if they would speak Latin, so I say that the
Muses would speak with Shakespeare's fine filed phrase, if they would
speak English."—(Meres's 'Palladis Tamia.')

Meres's "fine filed phrase" reminds us of Ben Jonson, when he
speaks of Shakespeare's " well turned and true filed lines."

whose "Palladis Tamia" we quote, was familiar not
only with what was being done in contemporary literature, but also with many of the authors of the day.
Not otherwise could he have gained his intimate knowledge of several works, which had not been published
when he wrote, as well as of some which were never
published at all. Many of the living poets of repute,
it is obvious, were personally known to him, and about
those who were not so known he was just the man to
seek out every piece of information within his reach.
Again and again he recurs to the name of Shakespeare
in a strain which proves how deep was the interest
he took both in the poet and his works. Possibly
he was a personal friend, but at least he had no
doubt, from what he knew and heard, that William
Shakespeare the actor was the author of the plays
as well as of the poems with which his name was
connected.

That Shakespeare's success as a furbisher-up of plays,
which wanted the magic of his hand to turn their dross
to gold, had, even before 1593, excited the jealousy of
at least one rival dramatist, is shown by the language
of Robert Greene in his "Groat's Worth of Wit, bought
with a Million of Repentance." Greene died in 1592,
leaving this tract behind him in manuscript. In it the

brilliant and at one time popular dramatist, sinking in
abject poverty into the grave, had poured out the
bitterness of his heart at seeing the players making a
rich harvest by acting pieces, while the authors of them,
like himself, were in poverty. His grudge against
Shakespeare was apparently intensified by the fact,
that the young man from Stratford not only acted
in plays, but wrote them, or, at least, had worked them
up for the stage.

"There is an upstart Crow," he writes, "beautified with
our feathers" (alluding apparently to plays originally written
by Greene and Marlowe, of which Shakespeare had somehow
or other made use), "that with his *Tyger's heart wrapt in a
player's hide*" (a parody of "Oh, Tyger's heart wrapt in a
woman's hide"—Shakespeare's 'Henry VI.,' part iii., act 1
sc. 4) "supposes he is as well able to bumbast out a blank
verse as the best of you; and, being an absolute *Johannes
Factotum*, is in his owne conceit the onely Shakescene in a
countrie."

A few months after Greene's death, in the same
year, 1592, the tract was published by his friend Henry
Chettle. It had given great offence to the "play-
makers" attacked in it; and as Greene could not be
attacked in return, Chettle, as sponsor for his tract,
found himself in the awkward position of having to

bear the responsibility for Greene's invective. Marlowe, to all appearance, and Shakespeare certainly,
considered themselves especially wronged; and to the
latter Chettle felt bound to make an apology, in an
" Address to the Gentlemen Readers," published in December 1592, along with his " Kind-Hart's Dreame."

" With neither of them that take offence," he writes, " was
I acquainted, and with one of them I care not if I never
be " (a very natural resolution, considering what a Bohemian
Marlowe was). " The other, whome at that time I did not
so much spare as since I wish I had, for that as I have
moderated the heate of living writers, and might have used
my owne discretion (especially in such a case), the Author
being dead, that I did not I am as sorry as if the originall
fault had been my fault, because myselfe have seene his
demeanour no lesse civill than he excellent in the quality
he professes. *Besides, divers of worship have reported his
uprightness of dealing, which argues his honesty, and his
facetious grace in writing, that approves his art.*"

It is therefore clear beyond all question, that so early
as 1592 Shakespeare had made a name for himself both
as actor and as author, " excellent in the quality he
professed," viz., acting, and noted for " facetious grace,"
or as we should now write, " graceful facility," in writing. The latter gift must have made him a most valu-

able member of the theatrical company to which he
belonged, and its possession was what, it is only reasonable to suppose, procured for him his rapid advancement
in the theatre. To polish up indifferent dialogue, to
write in effective speeches for his brother actors, to
recast inartistic plots, was work that must have been
constantly wanted in the theatre; and it is obviously
work which was frequently done by Shakespeare in
those early days. It was, moreover, a kind of work
that must often have been wanted in a hurry. It would
never have been intrusted to him unless his qualifications for it had been obvious. Would any man have
dared to undertake such work who had to trust to another man to do it for him? And if he did undertake
it, must not his brother actors have quickly found out
whether the work was his own or not? For much of
it must have had to be done under their own eye,
possibly within the theatre itself, conceived upon the
impulse of that quickness of invention, and executed
with that fluent facility, which a host of concurrent
testimony shows that his brother poets and actors
ascribed to Shakespeare as a distinguishing characteristic. Who can justly doubt that Webster, in the
preface to his " Victoria Corombona " (1612), was only
speaking of what was as apparent to all these as it was

to Webster himself, when he alluded to "the right happy
and copious industry of Mr Shakespeare "?

And yet the Baconians ask us to believe that not any
of the plays of which he was the recognised author
could have been written by him! Has it ever occurred
to them to reflect how inevitably a man reveals the
character and tendencies of his mind in his easy talk
with the friends who know him well, and whom he
trusts? Sir Walter Scott, anxious though he was to
keep secret even from his intimates the fact that he
wrote the Waverley Novels, could not, as we know,
help betraying it to such of them as were capable of
drawing a conclusion from the copious anecdotes and
distinctive humour with which his familiar conversa-
tion overflowed. Can it be supposed, then, if Shakespeare were the uncultured boor the Baconians assume
him to have been, that he would not have been found
out by his talk? Even in Goldsmith's case, Garrick's
well-known line—

" He wrote like an angel, and talked like poor Poll,"—

had in it more of playful sarcasm than of truth; for
are there not upon record many sayings of his which
were quite up to the level of the current talk of the
Literary Club? But whatever his talk, Goldsmith at

any rate was known by his friends to "write like an
angel"; and if Shakespeare could not write what he professed that he wrote, it is as certain as any deduction
from probabilities can be, that he could not have made
his way as he did among the poets and dramatists of the
day. Have the Baconians ever tried to picture to themselves what was the position of Shakespeare the actor
and accepted dramatic writer in a theatre of those days?
By necessity he was in daily communion with some of
the sharpest and finest intellects of the time. In the
theatre itself were men like Burbage, Armin, Taylor,
Lowine, Kempe, all well qualified to take the measure
of his capacity; while his profession as an actor, as well
as his pretensions as a writer of poetry and drama, must
have brought him into close contact, both at the theatre
and in their convivial gatherings, with men like Marlowe,
Dekker, Chapman, Middleton, Heywood, Drayton, and
Ben Jonson. We might as soon believe that a man
who pretended that he had written 'Vanity Fair' or
'Esmond,' but had not written them, could have escaped
detection in the society of Thackeray's friends, Charles
Buller, Tennyson, Venables, or James Spedding, as that
Shakespeare, without having written them, could have
passed himself off as the author of even "The Two
Gentlemen of Verona" or "Love's Labour's Lost"—we

purposely name two of his earliest and weakest plays,
—or that any of the brilliant circle of Elizabethan
poets would have given credit for ten minutes to such a
man as the Baconians picture Shakespeare to have been
for the capacity to construct one scene, or to compose
ten consecutive lines of the blank verse—the exquisite
blank verse—which is to be found in those plays.

Then, as the years flowed on, and the young poet of
the " Venus and Adonis " and the " Lucrece," who had
begun dramatic authorship by patching up old and inartistic plays well known to the public, put in his claim
to the nobler dramas which made him, in Ben Jonson's
words, " the wonder of our stage," is it to be supposed
that such rival writers as we have named could have
failed to see that it was the actor Shakespeare, their
chum and intimate companion, with all his marvellously
comprehensive grasp of character, his play of ebullient
humour, his unbounded exuberance of fancy and fer-
tility of exquisite expression, and none but he, whose
genius, and whose genius alone, breathed throughout
the series of dramas which, after 1592, were given to
the stage with a prodigality almost startling ?

By 1598, as we learn from Meres's ' Tamia,' already
cited, Shakespeare had established his claim to predomi-
nating excellence in both tragedy and comedy. " For

comedy, witness," says Meres, "his 'Gentlemen of
Verona,' his (Comedy of) 'Errors,' his 'Love's Labour
Lost,' his 'Love's Labour Wonne' (Much Ado), his
'Midsummer's Night Dream,' and his 'Merchant of
Venice'; for tragedy, his 'Richard II.,' 'Richard III.,'
'Henry IV.,' 'King John,' 'Titus Andronicus,' and his
'Romeo and Juliet.'". Within the ensuing twelve
years he had added to that noble list the other great
plays which will at once leap to every reader's memory.
If he had lived for fame, he might well think that by
this time he had lived enough for it. But what Florio
said of him was probably true, "that he loved better to
be a poet than to be called one." Most probably, too,
he had warnings within himself that the great fountain
of thought, imagination, and feeling, which had hitherto
flowed so copiously, was no longer to be relied on. The
wine of his poetic life had been drunk, and he was not
the man to wrong the public or his own reputation by
drawing upon the lees. *Tempus abire tibi est* was the
warning that was like enough to have come to a man
so wise, as it does evermore come to all thoughtful men.
He had made for himself what a man in whom the
elements were so temperately mingled was sure to
regard as a sufficient fortune; and to go back to his
boyhood's home and breathe again the free air of the

old familiar haunts, and share in the simple duties of
a well-to-do citizen among the ageing friends of his
early youth, was to such a nature a welcome release
from the anxieties and the conflicts of the crowded and
struggling and feverish life which had been his since
he started to seek his fortune in London. He had had
enough of the toil and turmoil there, and, like his own
Prospero, was glad

> " Thence to retire him to his Milan, where
> Every third thought should be his grave."

To London he obviously went after this upon
occasion,—partly on business, as we know; partly, it
may be presumed, to enjoy the stimulating society of
his old actor and literary friends. There he would
renew the wit-combats with Ben Jonson, of which
Thomas Fuller must have heard from living witnesses
of them,—for he could not have been present at them
in person,—when he wrote :—

" Which two I behold like a great Spanish Galleon and
an English Man-of-War; Master Jonson (like the former)
was built far higher in learning; solid, but slow in his per-
formances. Shakespeare, with the English Man-of-War,
lesser in bulk but lighter in sailing, could turn with all
tides, tack about, and take advantage of all winds, by the
quickness of his wit and invention."

Milton, also, though too young to have known Shakespeare, could scarcely fail to have spoken with many who
had seen and talked with him. Not else would he have
written of him as "my Shakespeare," or as "sweetest
Shakespeare, fancy's child." And now this well authen-
ticated repute of our poet in the circle where he was
best known is to be set aside, and we are asked to believe,
with Miss Delia Bacon and her followers, that Ben
Jonson, despite the frequent collision of their wits, was
unable to discover, what is so palpable to them, that
Shakespeare was a liar who throws Mendez Pinto into
the shade, and a literary impostor such as the world
has never dreamt of!

So far was Jonson from having a doubt as to the
works ascribed to Shakespeare being truly his, that in
his 'Timber; or, Discoveries upon Men and Matters,'
written long after Shakespeare was in his grave, he
described him in terms that confirm Fuller's estimate
in a remarkable degree:—

"He was (indeed) honest, and of an open and free nature;
had an excellent phantsie; brave notions and gentle expres-
sions; wherein he flowed with that facility, that sometimes
it was necessary he should be stop'd: *Sufflaminandus erat*,
as Augustus said of Haterius. His wit was in his power—
would the rule of it had been so too. . . . But he redeem'd

his [literary] vices with his virtues. There was ever more in him to be praysed than to be pardoned."

Who does not see, from this, the Shakespeare, not of the dramas merely but of social intercourse—with his flashes, not of merriment only, but also of pathos and of subtle thought, his flow of anecdote and whim playing like summer lightning amid the general talk of the room, and sometimes provoking the ponderous and irritable Jonson by throwing his sententious and learned talk into the shade? Brilliant talk would seem to have come to Shakespeare as easily as brilliant writing, and he would thus eclipse Jonson in society as he eclipsed him even when dealing with classical themes upon the stage. But the genial player and poet, to whom all concurred in giving the epithet of "gentle," was too good a fellow to deal in the wit that wounds, to presume on his personal popularity, or to view the efforts of a rival author with jealousy. Jonson had good cause to think well of him, for he had not in his early days hesitated to attack Shakespeare in very abusive terms;[1] and yet it was to Shakespeare's active intervention that he owed the production on the stage, by the Lord Chamberlain's company, of which Shakespeare was a member, of the fine play of

[1] See Appendix, p. 68.

"Every Man in his Humour," which Jonson, then in
needy circumstances, had failed to get them to accept.
This, and many other acts of good-fellowship, as well
as the numberless hours which the talk and fine spirits
of his friend had made memorable, were doubtless in
Jonson's mind, when, in a previous passage of the
'Memorandum' just quoted, he said of him, remem-
bering how kind, how generous, how free from self-
assertion he had been,—"I loved the man, and doe
honour his memory on this side idolatrie as much as
any." And this is the man we are now to be told
was the poor coarse-grained creature to which the
Baconians would reduce him !

In support of their theory they rest upon the cir-
cumstance that, after Shakespeare settled about 1612
in Stratford, no more plays appeared with his name.
If there had been anything extraordinary in that cir-
cumstance, surely Ben Jonson and his other author
friends would have been struck by it. We know that
down to the last he was in intimate contact with Jonson
and Michael Drayton, who, according to a fairly authen-
ticated tradition, visited him at Stratford about a month
before his death. But neither Jonson nor Drayton, nor,
what is more material, his player partners and intimates, hint anywhere the slightest surprise that he

ceased, while still in the vigour of his years, to furnish
the stage with fresh sources of attraction. Why he
so ceased no one can tell, any more than we can tell
with certainty why he did not himself see his works
through the press. He may very well have intended
to do this, so soon as they could be printed without in-
jury to the interests of the theatres to which he had
sold them, and to which it was important that they
should not be made available to rival theatres, as by
publication they would have been.

It must always be remembered, too, that Shakespeare
died of a sudden and brief illness, which probably cut
short many other projects besides that of having his
dramas printed in an authentic form. This view is
countenanced by the language of Heminges and Condell
in their dedication of the first folio to the Earls of Pembroke and Montgomery, in which they speak of Shakespeare with regret as "not having the fate common
with some, to be executor to his owne writings." To
them it seems clear enough that he would have brought
them out himself, had he lived. "We," they say, "have
but collected them, and done an office to the dead to
procure his orphanes guardians, *without ambition either
of selfe-profit or fame, onely to keep the memory of so
worthy a friend and fellow alive as was our Shakespeare,*

by humble offer of his playes to your most noble pa-
tronage." The words of their preface to the volume
are even more significant:—

"It had bene a thing, we confesse, worthy to have bene
wished, that the author himselfe had lived to have set forth
and overseen his own writings; but since it hath bin or-
dain'd otherwise, and he by death departed from that right,
we pray you do not envie his friends the office of their care
and pains to have collected and publish'd them; and so to
have publish'd them, as where (before) you were abus'd with
diverse stolne and surreptitious copies, maim'd and deform'd
by the frauds and stealthes of injurious impostors that ex-
pos'd them; even those are now offer'd to your view cur'd
and perfect of their limbes, and all the rest absolute in their
numbers as he conceiv'd them; *who, as he was a happie
imitator of Nature, was a most gentle expresser of it. His
mind and hand went together; and what he thought he uttered
with that easinesse, that we have scarce received from him a
blot in his papers.*"

Now who are the men who bear this testimony to the
fact that Shakespeare's "mind and hand went together," and that composition was to him so easy, that
his manuscripts—like Sir Walter Scott's, George Eliot's,
or Thackeray's, all great masters of style—were almost
without a blot? They were men who had been asso-
ciated with him for years as brother actors,—men who

must have often heard discussed in his presence what
plots were to be selected for new plays, and how they
were to be treated,—men who must have again and again
marked, with delighted surprise, how he had transformed
into something of which his fellows had never dreamed
the tales on which such plays as "The Merchant of
Venice," "Cymbeline," "The Winter's Tale," and "As You
Like It " were founded,—men who had known him from
time to time write in scenes and speeches, sometimes
of his own accord, but sometimes as likely at the suggestion of his brother actors, or at a rehearsal in their
very presence cut and carve upon a passage to give it
more point and finish. They at least knew his auto-
graph, and had seen his " papers." If he could not even
write his own name respectably, as the Baconians con-
tend, they must have known the fact, and would not
have ventured to speak of his " papers," when so many
people were alive, who, if the Baconians are right, could
have shown up the imposture. Remember, too, that this
very volume was dedicated to two noblemen of high
culture, the Earl of Pembroke and the Earl of Montgomery, who knew Shakespeare personally, and, in the
language of the Dedication, had treated both his plays
" and their author living " with much favour. Were such
men likely to have been the victims of a delusion ?

It in no way militates against the weight of this argument, that much of the first folio was a reprint merely of some of the plays which had already been printed in quarto. Heminges and Condell might not have intended by what they wrote to suggest that the book was entirely printed from his "papers." Their language may fairly be read merely as a record of the fact that the MSS. of his plays, as originally delivered by him to his "fellows" at the theatre, were not disfigured by the erasures and interlineations with which they were familiar in the MSS. of other dramatic writers.

Ben Jonson, it is true, thought this absence of blots no virtue in his friend. The players, he says, often mentioned it in Shakespeare's honour. "My answer hath beene, would he had blotted a thousand. . . . Many times he fell into those things could not escape laughter; as when he said in the person of Cæsar, one speaking to him,—*Cæsar, thou dost me wrong;* he reply'd, —*Cæsar did never wrong but with just cause;* and such like, which were ridiculous." There is a good deal to be said for the sentences excepted to by Jonson (which, by the way, are not in the first folio, nor indeed printed anywhere, though they may very possibly have been in Shakespeare's original MS.); but what Jonson writes is

of importance as showing that the cleanness and free-
dom from correction of Shakespeare's MSS. were notorious in the theatres to which he had belonged.

Jonson's deliberate thought as to how Shakespeare
worked, and that art as well as natural gifts went to
the composition of his works, is very clearly stated in
the splendid eulogy by him prefixed to the first folio:—

> " The merry Greek, tart Aristophanes,
> Neat Terence, witty Plautus, now not please,
> But antiquated and deserted lye,
> As they were not of Nature's family.
> Yet must I not give Nature all; thy art,
> My gentle Shakespeare, must enjoy a part;
> For though the poet's matter Nature be,
> His art doth give the fashion ! and that he,
> Who casts to write a living line must sweat,
> Such as thine are, and strike the second heat
> Upon the Muses anvile; turne the same
> And himselfe with it, that he thinkes to frame,
> Or for the laurell he may gaine a scorne,
> For a good poet's made as well as borne.
> AND SUCH WERT THOU ! "

Jonson was not the man to write thus without having
a basis of fact to go upon. What more natural than
that Shakespeare and he should have often talked over
passages in their plays, which one or the other thought
might be improved ? It may be, that among these pas-

sages were those very sentences in "Julius Cæsar" to
which we have seen that Jonson took exception; for in
the first folio ("Julius Cæsar," Act iii. sc. 1) what we
read is—

> " Know, Cæsar doth not wrong; nor without cause
> Will he be satisfied;"

—just such a correction as the Shakespeare described
by Heminges and Condell would be likely to make upon
the spur of the moment, if his attention had been called
to the seeming paradox of the words which Jonson
says he wrote.

Jonson had probably in his mind's eye many incidents of a similar nature, which satisfied him that all
the seeming artlessness of his friend—the "art without
art, unparalleled as yet," as the scholarly Leonard Digges
called it—was nothing more nor less than that highest
triumph of art, that perfection of simplicity and finish,
by which art is never suggested. No unprejudiced
mind can read what Jonson has written of Shakespeare
without having the conviction forced upon him, that
Jonson had seen in the man himself living and unmis-
takeable proofs, that in him was the genius from which
sprang both the poetry and the plays which were identified with his name. It is not of the plays alone, but

of the man also as he knew him, that Jonson was think-
ing, when he wrote the lines opposite the Droeshout
portrait in the first folio:—

> " Oh, could he [Droeshout] but have drawne his wit
> As well in brasse, as he hath hit
> His face, the print would then surpasse
> All that was ever writ in brasse."

And also in the lines—" To the memory of my beloved
the author, Mr William Shakespeare, *and what he hath
left us,*" apostrophising him as—

> " Soul of the age !
> " The applause ! delight ! the wonder of our stage !"

And again—

> " If I thought my judgement were of yeeres,"

—that is, that my opinion was to be prized by posterity—

> " I should commit thee surely with thy peers,
> And tell how far thou didst our Lily outshine,
> Or sporting Kyd, or Marlowe's mighty line.
> And though thou hadst small Latin and less Greeke,"

(How does this comport with the Baconians' theory of
the illiterate butcher's boy ?)

> " From thence to honour thee I would not seeke
> · For names, but call forth thund'ring Æschilus,
> Euripedes, and Sophocles to us,

Paccuvius, Accius, him of Cordova dead,
To life again, to hear thy buskin tread
And shake a stage ; or, when thy sockes were on,
Leave thee alone, for the comparison
Of all that insolent Greece, or haughtie Rome
Sent forth, or since did from their ashes come.
Triumph, my Britaine ! thou hast one to showe,
To whom all scenes of Europe homage owe.
He was not of an age, but for all time !"

There spoke out the heart of brave old Ben, remem-
bering how meekly the man with whose friendship he
had been blest had borne his honours, and had never
made him feel that all Jonson's "slow endeavouring
art," working even upon classic ground, could not bring
him abreast in popularity with the heaven-gifted man
who had "small Latin and less Greek." For so it was
in Ben Jonson's own time, as we learn from the lines
of Leonard Digges, who died in 1635 at the University
of Oxford, where he led a scholar's life, when he says,—

" So have I scene, when Cæsar would appeare,
And on the stage at half-sworde parley were
Brutus and Cassius, oh, how the audience
Were ravish'd ! With what wonder they went thence,
When some new day they would not brook a line
Of tedious (though well-labour'd) Catiline ;
Sejanus, too, was irksome ; they prized more
Honest Iago or the jealous Moore ;

> And though the Fox and subtell Alchimist,
> Long intermitted, could not quite be missed;
> Though these have shamed all th' ancients, and might raise
> Their author's merit with a crowne of bays;
> Yet these sometimes, even at a friend's desire,
> Acted, have scarce defray'd the seacoale fire
> And doore-keepers; when, let but Falstaffe come,
> Hal, Poins, the rest,—you scarce shall have a roome,
> All is so pester'd; let but Beatrice
> And Benedick be seene, loe, in a trice
> The cockpit, galleries, boxes, all are full."

Few men like the man who eclipses them in a race, where they think they are especially strong,—authors least of all. But "gentle" Shakespeare subdued the envy even of the rough and somewhat jealous Ben, who in the days when Shakespeare was a stranger to him, had attacked him with a rancour which only one so "gentle" as Shakespeare would have forgotten. But had Ben for a moment seen reason to surmise that the man who had so thoroughly distanced him and all his compeers in the arena of both tragedy and comedy was sailing under false colours, that he was "an upstart crow" wearing feathers not his own, it would not have been left for the Smiths, Bacons, Holmes, and Don-nellys of the nineteenth century to throw discredit upon the great name which from 1616 has been held in reverence by all cultivated men.

We have purposely refrained from entering upon any
of the arguments from the internal evidence of the
works of Shakespeare and Bacon, that Bacon did not
and could not have written the marvellous series of
plays of which until 1856 the authorship was undis-
puted. This would open a field far too wide for discussion. Life is short, and a conflict of æsthetic judg-
ments in such matters is, by its very nature, inter-
minable. Without, however, approaching the question
from the side of the plays, it may be worth while to
glance briefly at the evidence to be found in the Sonnets, that they at least were not from the same hand
as penned the famous Essays. That the best of what
are usually printed as Shakespeare's sonnets were acknowledged by people who knew him to be his genuine
work, admits of no doubt. It was a time when sonnets
were in high favour with lovers of poetry, and the
writers of them were numerous. We learn from other
examples that sonnets, whose authors were well known,
used to circulate freely in society, and that, as in Shakespeare's case, having got a reputation, they were put
into print by adventurous publishers without the priv-
ity of their authors.[1]   Shakespeare's efforts in this

---

[1] Thus W. Percy, in the "Address to the Reader" published in 1594
with his 'Sonnets to the Fairest Cœlia,' writes, "Whereas I was fully

department of poetry were, as we learn from Meres, well known to be his by his " friends," among whom they had been circulating for years before they were printed by G. Eld for T[homas] T[horpe] in 1609; and none of the Baconians, so far as we are aware, have ever ventured seriously to dispute the fact. To these sonnets, therefore, we may look with confidence as indicating the character of Shakespeare's mind and the distinctive qualities of his literary style,—the very same qualities, be it said in passing, as are conspicuous in the plays. If this be so, then they may be fairly contrasted with what we see of the same qualities in Bacon's more familiar compositions, and so help towards a judgment whether or not they sprang from the same mind.

Look, then, at Bacon's conception of womanhood as we find it in his essays. Is there in it a trace of romance, of the chivalrous reverence, of the passionate aspiration which inevitably find their way into the writings of every poetically-minded man where woman ⁻is the theme, and of which the Shakespeare sonnets are full ? On the contrary, Bacon's view of woman is essentially commonplace. To him she is, when at her

determined to have concealed my sonnets as things privy to myself, yet, of courtesy, having lent them to some, they were secretly committed to the press, and almost finished, before it came to my knowledge."

best, merely the good loyal housewife, the dutiful
minister to the desires, the comforts, and the wants of
the other sex. For beauty, no doubt, he had some
feeling, and spoke well of its "best part" as that
"which a picture cannot express"; and in the same
essay (that "Of Beauty"), he shows himself not in-
sensible to the charm of grace in motion and demeanour. But the beauty which was mainly present
to his mind was that *Beauté du Diable* which fascinates
the senses but leaves the heart and the imagination
untouched, — the beauty that, to use his own words,
"is as summer fruits, and cannot last." No hint shall
we anywhere discover of the feeling which finds voice
in Shakespeare's 104th Sonnet,—

> " To me, fair friend, you never can be old,
> For as you were, when first your eye I eyed,
> Such seems thy beauty still ! "

And yet Bacon was not thirty-five years old when his
essay "Of Beauty" was published,—a time of life when
the enthusiasm of love is perhaps strongest in a man
capable of the passion. Keeping this fact in view,
surely, if he were the poet we are now asked to believe
him to have been, one might expect to find in his essay
"Of Love," published at the same time, some of that

glow, some of that fine madness, which has always
been found to "possess the poet's brain" under the in-
fluence of this theme. But what is it that we do find?
"The stage," he says, "is more beholden to Love than
the Life of Man." But if this be true of the stage, why
is it true? Assuredly, because it is the passion that,
for good or evil, more than any other pervades life.

> "It is the very centre of the earth,
> Drawing all things to it ;"[1]—

and therefore naturally holds a prominent place upon
the stage, whose duty it is "to hold the mirror up to
nature." As the essay proceeds, it becomes plain that
Bacon had no higher conception of love than as an
evanescent material passion. It is, he says, "a weak
passion," out of which "great spirits keep,"—a thing
that is to be shunned, for it finds its way into "a heart
well fortified, if watch be not kept." The devout and
grateful humility of a noble love is to him no more
than "kneeling before a little idol,"—a making of one's
self "subject, though not of the mouth (as beasts are)
yet of the eye, which was given for higher purposes,"
—a something which men should "sever wholly from
their serious affairs and actions of life."

[1] "Troilus and Cressida," Act iv. sc. 2.

Now contrast this with the strain of sentiment which
inspires countless passages of the Sonnets, in which
hearts without number have found, and even in these
unromantic days evermore find delight, as expressing
the deepest, the purest, and most cherished feelings of
their lives. Then ask if the man who wrote of love as
Bacon wrote could have addressed to his mistress such
lines as—

> " My spirit is thine, the better part of me ! " [1]

> " So you are to my thoughts as food to life ; " [2]

or the Sonnet (the 29th) beginning—

> " When in disgrace with fortune and men's eyes ; "

or that (the 71st) beginning—

> " No longer mourn for me when I am dead ; "

with its lines of infinite pathos and beauty—

> " For I love you so,
> That I in your sweet thoughts would be forgot,
> If thinking of me then should make you woe."

Above all, could Bacon have penned that priceless creed
of all true lovers (the 116th Sonnet), beginning —

> " Let me not to the marriage of true minds
> Admit impediments,"

and ending—

[1] Sonnet 74.   [2] Sonnet 75.

" Love's not Time's fool, though rosy lips and cheeks
   Within his bending sickle's compass come ;
   Love alters not with his brief hours and weeks,
   But hears it out even to the edge of doom," &c.

From all we know either of Bacon's life or writings,
this and the multitude of similar passages which might
be quoted would have come within his censure, as but
"the speaking in a perpetual hyperbole, comely in
nothing but in love." But, indeed, how was it possible
that a man should write worthily of woman, or of that
love which is a love for evermore, who in his essay
"Of Marriage and Single Life" could find nothing
higher to say of wives than that they "are young
men's mistresses, companions for middle age, and old
men's nurses"? Idle to say, we are not to judge of a
man's prose by his poetry. Had Bacon been indeed a
poet, the feeling of exquisite tenderness, of profound
reverence for what is best in woman, which pervades
the Sonnets, must perforce have found its way into his
writings somewhere. Yet they will be ransacked in
vain for any indication of it.[1]

But it were idle to pursue the topic further; still
more idle to bring these and other writings of Bacon
to the test of a comparison with the plays, and to

[1] See note, "A Baconian on Shakespeare's Women," Appendix, p. 69.

contrast his grave, square - cut, antithetical, ponderous, unemotional style, and the absence in them of
everything like dramatic imagination and humour,
with the exuberance of poetical imagery and illustration, the variety of rhythmical cadence, the ex-
quisitely modulated flow of aptly balanced diction,
not to speak of the creative dramatic power, and
the buoyant play of irrepressible humour and wit,
which brighten even the slightest of the Shakespearian plays. This would demand an essay of itself,
which no one competent to write it will deem otherwise than superfluous, until better reason is shown
than has yet been shown for setting up Bacon's claim
to the imagination which "bodies forth the forms of
things unseen," and which would alone have enabled
him to conceive and place living before us such beings
as Macbeth, Othello, King Lear, Jack Falstaff, Imogen,
Hermione, Rosalind, and all the other glorious figures
of that marvellous gallery.

Our task is of a much humbler kind. We have purposely confined ourselves to a naked statement of facts
as to the man Shakespeare, based upon contemporary
testimony, and argued from upon the principles which
guide the judgment of practical men in all matters,
where they have only contemporary evidence from

which to draw their conclusions. On what better evidence than we have cited in regard to Shakespeare, do we believe that Æschylus, Sophocles, and Euripides wrote the plays coupled with their names, that Horace wrote his Odes, or Tacitus his Germania? From the belief of three centuries the world is not to be shaken by the fine-spun theories of men who, judging by all they write, know nothing of the mysterious ways in which genius works, and who conceive that fine poetry, and a sweep of thought, of invention, and of knowledge of the human heart, vast beyond their limited conceptions, can only issue from the brain of a man trained in the learning of the schools and moving in high society. Something more than conjecture, something more than unwarrantable assumption, must be produced to entitle them even to a hearing, however slight, at this time of day.

But now we are told that the true authorship of the pseudo-Shakespearian works has been established by a great American discoverer, Mr Ignatius Donnelly, a lawyer, ex-member of Congress, and ex-senator of Minnesota, who conceives that he has solved the problem in a work bearing the name of ' The Great Cryptogram : Francis Bacon's Cipher in the so-called Shakespeare Plays.' As if the man who had written

the thirty-six plays of the first folio would have left
to the chance of a cryptogram being deciphered three
centuries after his death the discovery of the fact that
he had written them!

We gather from his book that Mr Donnelly, lawyer
though he be, and by his profession bound to have
some regard to the laws of evidence, started upon his
investigations with the fixed idea that Shakespeare's
name was simply a mask for Bacon. He does not
commend himself to much consideration when we
find that he adopts as gospel, and with a vehemence
that wholly discredits his judgment, all the preposterous nonsense of previous Baconians about Shakespeare having had no education, of his having been a
tavern-haunter and habitual poacher, a mere money-
grubbing usurer, who could not spell his own name,
and who was glad to get back to Stratford to his
old occupation of butcher and wool-stapler, having
had his purse previously well lined by Bacon for
having lent the use of his name to a scandalous
fraud for some twenty odd years. Neither does he
prepossess us in his favour,—although of his sincerity
we entertain no doubt,—when he tells us that he was
put upon the trail of his vaunted discovery by coming
across an elaborate cipher of Bacon's, quoted in 'Every

Boy's Book.' " Then," he says, " followed like a flash
this thought, could Bacon have put a cipher in his
plays?" On further inquiry, he found, what is very
well known, that Bacon had a fancy for cryptographic
systems which "elude and exclude the decipherers."
Upon this hint Mr Donnelly set to work to find out a
cipher in the first folio edition of the plays that was to
confirm his preconceived theory, and, of course, he
found it to his own satisfaction. If, however, any
judgment may be formed as to the results of his hunt
from the specimens he has published, a more thorough
illustration can scarcely be conceived of the process
known as elucidating the *obscurum* by the *obscurius*.
There will no doubt be found persons, blessed or
cursed, as it may be, with such superabundance of time
upon their hands, and with a passion for such a literary
wild-goose chase as Mr Donnelly invites them to, that
they will follow him through arbitrary mazes of figures
and calculations which would drive any ordinary brain
mad, and which leads up to conclusions no less fantastic.

On such a chase, however, we do not conceive that
Mr Donnelly has a right to ask any one to enter until
he can first establish from credible evidence the following propositions: (1) That Bacon did in some clear and
unmistakable way set up in his life a claim to the

work which has hitherto been assigned to Shakespeare;
(2) That he was privy to the publication of the first
folio; (3) That he had Heminges and Condell under his
thumb, and got them to write what they did write in
the Dedication and Preface, with the deliberate purpose
of throwing the world off the scent as to the real
authorship; (4) That he suborned Ben Jonson to become a party to the fraud; (5) That there exists somewhere, and in some definite form under Bacon's hand,
a suggestion, no matter how slight, to lead posterity to
believe that in due time the composition of the plays
would be demonstrated to have been falsely assigned to
Shakespeare, and to be due entirely to himself.

When a satisfactory answer is given on these points,
then, but not till then, Mr Donnelly may have some
excuse for intruding his so-called discovery upon the
public. But upon them his two portentous volumes
are absolutely silent. It is idle to tell us, as he and
his predecessors do, that Bacon had reason during his
life to conceal his connection with the stage. It is an
assumption without warrant either in fact or probability. If Bacon gave his name to masques, why
should he have hesitated to give it to "Macbeth"
or "Julius Cæsar"? Moreover, no man who wrote
the plays assigned to Shakespeare could have kept

up such an imposture for such a lengthened period,
and under the very peculiar circumstances in which
these were produced — one of them, "The Merry
Wives of Windsor," written at Queen Elizabeth's
request and produced within a fortnight. But grant
that there might be reason for concealment while
Bacon was alive, there could be none after his death.
He might say of himself then, in the words of his
own (?) Macbeth—

> "After life's fitful fever I sleep well,
> Nothing can touch me further."

By that time he would be beyond reach of the anger of
either "Eliza or our James," who, in common with their
subjects, shared the general belief in the genius of
Shakespeare. How simple a matter, then, would it
have been to place upon record, *along with the requisite
proofs — for clear proof would in any case have been
wanted* — that he, and not Shakespeare, wrote the
plays ! Write them if he did, is it conceivable that
he would not have been so proud of their authorship
that he would have taken care to place the fact beyond a doubt, and to enjoin his executors to have jus-
tice done to his claim ?
This he unquestionably did not do, and yet we are

asked to give a hearing to an American lawyer, who, nearly three centuries after Bacon's death, chooses first to imagine that Bacon wrote the immortal plays, and then to assure us that, instead of placing the fact upon record, as any man of common-sense would be sure to place it, he wrapt up his secret in a cryptogram, *of which he did not even leave the key*—a cryptogram distributed in a most mystical and bewildering way through the bad printing of the first folio, and which it was left for Mr Donnelly's laborious and perverted ingenuity to discover!

Mr Donnelly and his proselytes would have us forget that Bacon knew what was evidence, and what was not, far too well to trust to a cryptogram for the establishment of so important a fact as that he was entitled to the fame which he knew the plays in question had won for the Stratford poet. However clear a cryptogram might be, it could not, as he very well knew, possibly amount to more than a mere assertion by an interested witness. On the assumption of fraud on Shakespeare's part, it was a fraud of which Bacon himself was the instigator. He had helped, *ex hypothesi*, to set up Shakespeare's claim, and he of all men must have known that, his own testimony being radically tainted, this claim could only be displaced either by conclusive extraneous evidence, or by the confession of Shakespeare himself.

Again we say, no man has a right, without a sure ground of fact to go upon, to strain our credulity as Mr Donnelly does, or to ask reasonable men to investigate the cumbrous processes by which he works out his "Great Cryptogram" theory. Let Mr Donnelly get over the initial difficulties which we have suggested, and then Shakespearian students will give him a hearing. Till then, they, and all men who recognise that one of life's chief responsibilities is the responsibility for a right use of our time, will be content to abide in the faith of Shakespeare's contemporaries, and of wellnigh three centuries of rational men, that the kindly and modest man, whose mortal remains rest in front of the altar in Stratford Church, was no impostor, but the veritable author of the works for which, as one of its wholly priceless possessions, the civilised world owes to him endless gratitude.

APPENDIX.

NOTE TO p. 17.

SPECIMENS OF BACON'S POETRY.

THE only verses which beyond all doubt are known to have been written by Bacon are his versions of seven of the Psalms of David. They were written about two years before his death, and must therefore be taken as showing whatever mastery he had attained by previous practice over our language for poetical purposes. Admit the postulate of Miss Bacon and her followers, that he wrote all for which an ignorant world has given Shakespeare credit, and then judge if such a verse as the following was likely to have flowed from the pen of the author of the "Venus and Adonis," of the best of the Sonnets, or of "Cymbeline" or "Hamlet":—

> "Who sows in tears shall reap in joy,
>   The Lord doth so ordain ;
> So that his seed be pure and good,
>   His harvest shall he gain."
>   —Psalm cxxvi. 5.

Or this as the rendering from the 90th Psalm of the words,
"Thou hast set our iniquities before Thee : our secret sins
in the light of Thy countenance":—

> "Thou buriest not within Oblivion's tomb
> Our trespasses, but enterest them aright ;
> Even those that are conceived in darkness' womb
> To Thee appear as done at broad daylight."

Now see how the dominant thought in each of these
stanzas has been treated by Shakespeare,—the first in
"Richard III.," iv. 4, and the second in "Hamlet," iii. 3 :—

> "The liquid drops of tears that you have shed
> Shall come again, transformed to orient pearls,
> Advantaging their loan with interest,
> Oftentimes double gain of happiness."

> "'Tis not so above :
> There is no shuffling, there the action lies
> In his true nature : and we ourselves compelled,
> Even in the teeth and forehead of your faith,
> To give in evidence."[1]

Could the same man have written these passages and the
hidebound stanzas of Bacon's "Psalms"? Here and there
a good line occurs in some of these translations, just as
Hobbes in his version of the 'Iliad' now and then struck
out a line of genuine poetry. But they are such as no man

---

[1] The contrast between Bacon and Shakespeare in these two passages was first pointed out in the first of two admirable lectures on the
"Bacon-Shakespeare Controversy," by Charles H. Higgins, M.D., published in Liverpool in 1886.

would have written who possessed a genuine poetical gift,
or the command of poetical and musical language, which
the practice of rhythmical composition must have produced.
They will be found in Mr Spedding's edition of Bacon's
works, vol. vii. pp. 273-286.

To Bacon has been attributed, on no sufficient evidence,
the following poem, which it is said he wrote for Lord
Burleigh:—

THE RETIRED COURTIER.

His golden locks hath Time to silver turned;
  O Time too swift! O swiftness never ceasing!
His youth 'gainst Time and Age hath ever spurned,
  But spurned in vain: youth waneth by increasing;
Beauty, strength, youth, are flowers but fading seeme;
Duty, faith, love, are roots and ever greene.

His helmet now shall make a hive for bees,
  And lover's sonnets turn to holy psalmes;
A man-at-arms must now serve on his knees,
  And feed on praiers which are Age's Almes;
But though from Court to College he depart,
His saint is sure of his unspotted heart.

And when he saddest sits in homely cell,
  He'll teach his swaines this carol for a song:
Blest be the hearts that wish my sovereign well!
  Curst be the soul that thinks her any wrong!
Goddess, allow this aged man his right
To be your headsman now, that was your knight.

E

This poem, which appeared without the author's name in
Dowland's 'First Book of Songs,' published in 1600, will
not go far to establish a reputation as a poet for whoever
wrote it. It is more likely to be held in memory from
being quoted by Thackeray and applied to Colonel New-
come in one of the last chapters of 'The Newcomes,' than
from any intrinsic merit.

Mr Donnelly and others claim the following poem for
Bacon. Mr Spedding admits that it may possibly be his.
It is a laboured expansion rather than a paraphrase of a
Greek epigram, variously attributed to Poseidippus, to Plato
the comic poet, and to Crates the Cynic. It matters little
to whom the original Greek is due. Most certainly no one
will claim it for Shakespeare, false as it is in philosophy,
false in sentiment,—the protest of a sour and commonplace
mind against the Creator's dealings with His creatures. It
may be called

LIFE A CURSE.

The world's a bubble, and the life of man
        Less than a span ;
In his conception wretched, from the womb
        So to the tomb ;
Cursed from his cradle and brought up to years
        With cares and fears :
Who, then, to frail mortality shall trust
But limns the water, or but writes in dust.

Yet, whilst with sorrow here we live opprest,
    What life is best ?
Courts are but only superficial schools,
    To dandle fools ;
The rural parts are turned into a den
    Of savage men ;
And where's the city from foul vice so free,
But may be termed the worst of all the three ?

Domestic cares afflict the husband's bed,
    Or pains his head.
Those that live single take it for a curse,
    Or do things worse.
Some would have children : those that have them moan,
    Or wish them gone.
What is it, then, to have or have no wife,
But single thraldom or a double strife ?

Our own affections still at home to please
    Is a disease :
To cross the seas to any foreign soil,
    Perils and toil.
Wars with their noise affright us ; when they cease,
    We're worse in peace.
What then remains, but that we still should cry,
Not to be born, or, being born, to die ?

Note to p. 37.

BEN JONSON'S SCURRILOUS SONNET ON SHAKESPEARE.

ON POET APE.

Poor poet Ape, that would be thought our chief,
 Whose works are e'en the frippery of wit,
From brokage has become so bold a thief,
 That we, the robbed, have rage and pity it.
At first he made low shifts, would pick and glean,
 Buy the reversion of old plays ; now grown
To a little wealth and credit in the scene,
 He takes up all—makes each man's wit his own,
And told of this he slights it.—Tut ! Such crimes
 The sluggish gaping auditor devours ;
He marks not whose 'twas first, and after-times
 May judge it to be his as well as ours.
Fool ! As if half eyes will not know a fleece
From locks of wool, or shreds from the whole piece !

This is quite in the vein of Richard Greene's attack on Shakespeare. But it has an incidental value as showing that Jonson, when he wrote it, shared the universal belief of Shakespeare's intimates and acquaintances, that he, and nobody else, dressed up and put new life into old and faulty plays, and made them popular in their altered form.

NOTE TO p. 53.

A BACONIAN ON SHAKESPEARE'S WOMEN.

The Baconians obviously feel the pinch of the line of argument in the text, for they are driven to meet it by alleging that Shakespeare's plays show that the writer of them had as low an estimate of women as Bacon. Thus Mrs Potts, in a note (p. 479) to her edition of Bacon's " Promus " (London, 1883), says :—

" From the entries which refer to women we see that Bacon formed very unfavourable views regarding them,— views which unhappy passages in his own life probably tended to confirm. *The Shakespeare plays seem to exhibit the same unfavourable sentiments of their author.* There are 130 female personages in the plays, and the characters of these seem to be easily divisible into six classes :—

" 1. Furies or viragos, such as Tamora, Queen Margaret, Goneril, Regan, and even Lady Macbeth in the dark side of her character.

" 2. Shrews and sharp-tongued women, as Katharine, Constance, and many others, when they are represented as angry.

" 3. Gossiping and untrustworthy women, as most of the maids, hostesses, &c., and as Percy insinuates that he considers his wife to be.

" 4. Fickle, faithless, and artful — a disposition which seems assumed throughout the plays to be the normal condition of womanhood (!).

" 5. Thoroughly immoral, as Cleopatra, Phrynia, Timandra, Bianca.

" 6. Gentle, simple, and colourless, as Hero, Olivia, Ophelia, Cordelia, &c.

" Noteworthy exceptions, which exhibit more exalted and finer pictures of good and noble women, are the characters of Isabella, Volumnia, and of Katharine of Aragon ; but these are not sufficient to do away with the impression that, *on the whole, the author of the plays had but a poor opinion of women ; that love he regarded as youthful passion, marriage as a doubtful happiness.*"

Every man or woman who has made a study of Shakespeare can estimate for him or herself what weight is to be attached to the judgment which could arrive at such conclusions.

THE END.

PRINTED BY WILLIAM BLACKWOOD AND SONS.

www.ingramcontent.com/pod-product-compliance
Lightning Source LLC
Chambersburg PA
CBHW021524270326
41930CB00008B/1075